>>>————————————————<<<

THIS BOOK BELONGS TO

>>>————————————————<<<

BOAT

CAPTAIN

ENGINE HOURS

FUEL

CREW

- •
- •
- •
- •
- •
- •

PORT OF DEPARTURE

LOCATION

DATE

TIME

DISTANCE	DURATION

PORT OF DESTINATION

LOCATION

DATE

TIME

PORT INDEX

DOCKMASTER

PHONE

MAIL

DOCKING FEES

SLIP #

SPECIAL FEATURES

WEATHER CONDITIONS

SEA STRENGTH

CALM   1   2   3   4   5   ROUGH

ADDITIONAL NOTES

LOGGED BY

BOAT

CAPTAIN

ENGINE HOURS

FUEL

CREW

•	•
•	•
•	•

PORT OF DEPARTURE

LOCATION

DATE

TIME

DISTANCE	DURATION

WEATHER CONDITIONS

SEA STRENGTH

CALM 1 2 3 4 5 ROUGH

PORT OF DESTINATION

LOCATION

DATE

TIME

PORT INDEX

DOCKMASTER

PHONE

MAIL

DOCKING FEES

SLIP #

SPECIAL FEATURES

ADDITIONAL NOTES

LOGGED BY

BOAT

CAPTAIN

ENGINE HOURS

FUEL

CREW

•	•
•	•
•	•

PORT OF DEPARTURE

LOCATION

DATE

TIME

DISTANCE	DURATION

WEATHER CONDITIONS

SEA STRENGTH

	1	2	3	4	5	
CALM	○	○	○	○	○	ROUGH

PORT OF DESTINATION

LOCATION

DATE

TIME

PORT INDEX

DOCKMASTER

PHONE

MAIL

DOCKING FEES

SLIP #

SPECIAL FEATURES

ADDITIONAL NOTES

LOGGED BY

BOAT

CAPTAIN

ENGINE HOURS

FUEL

CREW

•	•
•	•
•	•

PORT OF DEPARTURE

LOCATION

DATE

TIME

DISTANCE	DURATION

WEATHER CONDITIONS

SEA STRENGTH

CALM 1 2 3 4 5 ROUGH

PORT OF DESTINATION

LOCATION

DATE

TIME

PORT INDEX

DOCKMASTER

PHONE

MAIL

DOCKING FEES

SLIP #

SPECIAL FEATURES

ADDITIONAL NOTES

LOGGED BY

⛵ BOAT

⚙️ CAPTAIN

🕐 ENGINE HOURS

🛢️ FUEL

CREW

•	•
•	•
•	•

PORT OF DEPARTURE

| 📍 LOCATION |
| 📅 DATE |
| 🕐 TIME |

DISTANCE	DURATION

PORT OF DESTINATION

| 📍 LOCATION |
| 📅 DATE |
| 🕐 TIME |

PORT INDEX

| 🏃 DOCKMASTER |
| 📞 PHONE |
| ✉️ MAIL |
| 💲 DOCKING FEES |
| ⚓ SLIP # |
| 🎖️ SPECIAL FEATURES |

WEATHER CONDITIONS

🌡️ —— ☀️ ⛅ 🌧️ ⛈️ ❄️

🚩 —— ☐ ☐ ☐ ☐ ☐

SEA STRENGTH

〰️ CALM ○1 ○2 ○3 ○4 ○5 〰️ ROUGH

ADDITIONAL NOTES

LOGGED BY

BOAT

CAPTAIN

ENGINE HOURS

FUEL

CREW

•	•
•	•
•	•

PORT OF DEPARTURE

LOCATION

DATE

TIME

DISTANCE	DURATION

WEATHER CONDITIONS

SEA STRENGTH

CALM 1 2 3 4 5 ROUGH

PORT OF DESTINATION

LOCATION

DATE

TIME

PORT INDEX

DOCKMASTER

PHONE

MAIL

DOCKING FEES

SLIP #

SPECIAL FEATURES

ADDITIONAL NOTES

LOGGED BY

BOAT

CAPTAIN

ENGINE HOURS

FUEL

CREW

•	•
•	•
•	•

PORT OF DEPARTURE

LOCATION

DATE

TIME

DISTANCE	DURATION

WEATHER CONDITIONS

☀ ⛅ 🌧 ⛈ ❄

☐ ☐ ☐ ☐ ☐

SEA STRENGTH

CALM	1	2	3	4	5	ROUGH
	○	○	○	○	○	

PORT OF DESTINATION

LOCATION

DATE

TIME

PORT INDEX

DOCKMASTER

PHONE

MAIL

DOCKING FEES

SLIP #

SPECIAL FEATURES

ADDITIONAL NOTES

LOGGED BY

BOAT

CAPTAIN

ENGINE HOURS

FUEL

CREW

.	.
.	.
.	.

PORT OF DEPARTURE

LOCATION

DATE

TIME

DISTANCE	DURATION

WEATHER CONDITIONS

SEA STRENGTH

CALM 1 2 3 4 5 ROUGH

PORT OF DESTINATION

LOCATION

DATE

TIME

PORT INDEX

DOCKMASTER

PHONE

MAIL

DOCKING FEES

SLIP #

SPECIAL FEATURES

ADDITIONAL NOTES

LOGGED BY

BOAT

CAPTAIN

ENGINE HOURS

FUEL

CREW

•	•
•	•
•	•

PORT OF DEPARTURE

LOCATION

DATE

TIME

DISTANCE	DURATION

WEATHER CONDITIONS

SEA STRENGTH

CALM 1 2 3 4 5 ROUGH

PORT OF DESTINATION

LOCATION

DATE

TIME

PORT INDEX

DOCKMASTER

PHONE

MAIL

DOCKING FEES

SLIP #

SPECIAL FEATURES

ADDITIONAL NOTES

LOGGED BY

BOAT

CAPTAIN

ENGINE HOURS

FUEL

CREW

·	·
·	·
·	·

PORT OF DEPARTURE

LOCATION

DATE

TIME

DISTANCE	DURATION

WEATHER CONDITIONS

SEA STRENGTH

CALM 1 2 3 4 5 ROUGH

PORT OF DESTINATION

LOCATION

DATE

TIME

PORT INDEX

DOCKMASTER

PHONE

MAIL

DOCKING FEES

SLIP #

SPECIAL FEATURES

ADDITIONAL NOTES

LOGGED BY

BOAT

CAPTAIN

ENGINE HOURS

FUEL

CREW

•	•
•	•
•	•

PORT OF DEPARTURE

LOCATION

DATE

TIME

DISTANCE	DURATION

WEATHER CONDITIONS

☀ ⛅ 🌧 ⛈ ❄

☐ ☐ ☐ ☐ ☐

SEA STRENGTH

CALM 1 2 3 4 5 ROUGH

PORT OF DESTINATION

LOCATION

DATE

TIME

PORT INDEX

DOCKMASTER

PHONE

MAIL

DOCKING FEES

SLIP #

SPECIAL FEATURES

ADDITIONAL NOTES

LOGGED BY

BOAT

CAPTAIN

ENGINE HOURS

FUEL

CREW

•	•
•	•
•	•

PORT OF DEPARTURE

LOCATION

DATE

TIME

DISTANCE	DURATION

WEATHER CONDITIONS

🌡 ——	☼	⛅	🌧	⛈	❄
——	☐	☐	☐	☐	☐

SEA STRENGTH

CALM 1 2 3 4 5 ROUGH

PORT OF DESTINATION

LOCATION

DATE

TIME

PORT INDEX

DOCKMASTER

PHONE

MAIL

DOCKING FEES

SLIP #

SPECIAL FEATURES

ADDITIONAL NOTES

LOGGED BY

⚓ BOAT		CREW

⚓ BOAT
⚙ CAPTAIN
⏱ ENGINE HOURS
🛢 FUEL

CREW	
•	•
•	•
•	•

PORT OF DEPARTURE

📍 LOCATION
📅 DATE
🕐 TIME

DISTANCE	DURATION

PORT OF DESTINATION

📍 LOCATION
📅 DATE
🕐 TIME

PORT INDEX

🏃 DOCKMASTER
📞 PHONE
✉ MAIL
💰 DOCKING FEES
⚓ SLIP #
🎖 SPECIAL FEATURES

WEATHER CONDITIONS

🌡 ____   ☀ ⛅ 🌧 ⛈ ❄

🚩 ____   ☐ ☐ ☐ ☐ ☐

SEA STRENGTH

CALM 1 ◯ 2 ◯ 3 ◯ 4 ◯ 5 ◯ ROUG

ADDITIONAL NOTES

LOGGED BY

BOAT

CAPTAIN

ENGINE HOURS

FUEL

CREW

•	•
•	•
•	•

PORT OF DEPARTURE

LOCATION

DATE

TIME

DISTANCE	DURATION

WEATHER CONDITIONS

SEA STRENGTH

CALM	1	2	3	4	5	ROUGH

PORT OF DESTINATION

LOCATION

DATE

TIME

PORT INDEX

DOCKMASTER

PHONE

MAIL

DOCKING FEES

SLIP #

SPECIAL FEATURES

ADDITIONAL NOTES

LOGGED BY

BOAT

CAPTAIN

ENGINE HOURS

FUEL

CREW

•	•
•	•
•	•

PORT OF DEPARTURE

LOCATION

DATE

TIME

DISTANCE	DURATION

WEATHER CONDITIONS

SEA STRENGTH

CALM   1   2   3   4   5   ROUGH

PORT OF DESTINATION

LOCATION

DATE

TIME

PORT INDEX

DOCKMASTER

PHONE

MAIL

DOCKING FEES

SLIP #

SPECIAL FEATURES

ADDITIONAL NOTES

LOGGED BY

BOAT

CAPTAIN

ENGINE HOURS

FUEL

CREW

•	•
•	•
•	•

PORT OF DEPARTURE

LOCATION

DATE

TIME

DISTANCE	DURATION

WEATHER CONDITIONS

SEA STRENGTH

	1	2	3	4	5	
CALM	○	○	○	○	○	ROUGH

PORT OF DESTINATION

LOCATION

DATE

TIME

PORT INDEX

DOCKMASTER

PHONE

MAIL

DOCKING FEES

SLIP #

SPECIAL FEATURES

ADDITIONAL NOTES

LOGGED BY

BOAT

CAPTAIN

ENGINE HOURS

FUEL

CREW

- •
- •
- •
- •
- •
- •

PORT OF DEPARTURE

LOCATION

DATE

TIME

DISTANCE	DURATION

PORT OF DESTINATION

LOCATION

DATE

TIME

PORT INDEX

DOCKMASTER

PHONE

MAIL

DOCKING FEES

SLIP #

SPECIAL FEATURES

WEATHER CONDITIONS

SEA STRENGTH

CALM   1   2   3   4   5   ROUG

ADDITIONAL NOTES

LOGGED BY

BOAT

CAPTAIN

ENGINE HOURS

FUEL

CREW

•	•
•	•
•	•

PORT OF DEPARTURE

LOCATION

DATE

TIME

DISTANCE	DURATION

WEATHER CONDITIONS

SEA STRENGTH

CALM 1 2 3 4 5 ROUGH

PORT OF DESTINATION

LOCATION

DATE

TIME

PORT INDEX

DOCKMASTER

PHONE

MAIL

DOCKING FEES

SLIP #

SPECIAL FEATURES

ADDITIONAL NOTES

LOGGED BY

BOAT

CAPTAIN

ENGINE HOURS

FUEL

CREW

•	•
•	•
•	•

PORT OF DEPARTURE

LOCATION

DATE

TIME

DISTANCE	DURATION

WEATHER CONDITIONS

☀ ⛅ 🌧 ⛈ ❄

☐ ☐ ☐ ☐ ☐

SEA STRENGTH

	1	2	3	4	5	
CALM	○	○	○	○	○	ROUGH

PORT OF DESTINATION

LOCATION

DATE

TIME

PORT INDEX

DOCKMASTER

PHONE

MAIL

DOCKING FEES

SLIP #

SPECIAL FEATURES

ADDITIONAL NOTES

LOGGED BY

BOAT

CAPTAIN

ENGINE HOURS

FUEL

CREW

•	•
•	•
•	•

PORT OF DEPARTURE

LOCATION

DATE

TIME

DISTANCE	DURATION

WEATHER CONDITIONS

SEA STRENGTH

CALM 1 2 3 4 5 ROUGH

PORT OF DESTINATION

LOCATION

DATE

TIME

PORT INDEX

DOCKMASTER

PHONE

MAIL

DOCKING FEES

SLIP #

SPECIAL FEATURES

ADDITIONAL NOTES

LOGGED BY

⛵ **BOAT**
⚙️ **CAPTAIN**
🕐 **ENGINE HOURS**
🛢️ **FUEL**

CREW

•	•
•	•
•	•

PORT OF DEPARTURE

📍 LOCATION
📅 DATE
🕐 TIME

DISTANCE	DURATION

WEATHER CONDITIONS

🌡️ ——   ☀️ ⛅ 🌧️ ⛈️ ❄️

🏴 ——   ☐ ☐ ☐ ☐ ☐

SEA STRENGTH

CALM	1	2	3	4	5	ROUG
	○	○	○	○	○	

PORT OF DESTINATION

📍 LOCATION
📅 DATE
🕐 TIME

PORT INDEX

🏃 DOCKMASTER
📞 PHONE
✉️ MAIL
💲 DOCKING FEES
⚓ SLIP #
🎖️ SPECIAL FEATURES

ADDITIONAL NOTES

LOGGED BY

BOAT

CAPTAIN

ENGINE HOURS

FUEL

CREW

•	•
•	•
•	•

PORT OF DEPARTURE

LOCATION

DATE

TIME

DISTANCE	DURATION

WEATHER CONDITIONS

SEA STRENGTH

CALM	1	2	3	4	5	ROUGH

PORT OF DESTINATION

LOCATION

DATE

TIME

PORT INDEX

DOCKMASTER

PHONE

MAIL

DOCKING FEES

SLIP #

SPECIAL FEATURES

ADDITIONAL NOTES

LOGGED BY

BOAT

CAPTAIN

ENGINE HOURS

FUEL

CREW

- •
- •
- •
- •
- •
- •

PORT OF DEPARTURE

LOCATION

DATE

TIME

DISTANCE	DURATION

WEATHER CONDITIONS

SEA STRENGTH

CALM 1 2 3 4 5 ROUGH

PORT OF DESTINATION

LOCATION

DATE

TIME

PORT INDEX

DOCKMASTER

PHONE

MAIL

DOCKING FEES

SLIP #

SPECIAL FEATURES

ADDITIONAL NOTES

LOGGED BY

BOAT

CAPTAIN

ENGINE HOURS

FUEL

CREW	
•	•
•	•
•	•

PORT OF DEPARTURE

LOCATION

DATE

TIME

DISTANCE	DURATION

WEATHER CONDITIONS

SEA STRENGTH

| CALM | 1 | 2 | 3 | 4 | 5 | ROUGH |

PORT OF DESTINATION

LOCATION

DATE

TIME

PORT INDEX

DOCKMASTER

PHONE

MAIL

DOCKING FEES

SLIP #

SPECIAL FEATURES

ADDITIONAL NOTES

LOGGED BY

BOAT

CAPTAIN

ENGINE HOURS

FUEL

CREW

·	·
·	·
·	·

PORT OF DEPARTURE

- LOCATION
- DATE
- TIME

DISTANCE	DURATION

WEATHER CONDITIONS

SEA STRENGTH

CALM 1 2 3 4 5 ROUGH

PORT OF DESTINATION

- LOCATION
- DATE
- TIME

PORT INDEX

- DOCKMASTER
- PHONE
- MAIL
- DOCKING FEES
- SLIP #
- SPECIAL FEATURES

ADDITIONAL NOTES

LOGGED BY

BOAT

CAPTAIN

ENGINE HOURS

FUEL

CREW

•	•
•	•
•	•

PORT OF DEPARTURE

LOCATION

DATE

TIME

DISTANCE	DURATION

WEATHER CONDITIONS

SEA STRENGTH

CALM	1	2	3	4	5	ROUGH

PORT OF DESTINATION

LOCATION

DATE

TIME

PORT INDEX

DOCKMASTER

PHONE

MAIL

DOCKING FEES

SLIP #

SPECIAL FEATURES

ADDITIONAL NOTES

LOGGED BY

BOAT

CAPTAIN

ENGINE HOURS

FUEL

CREW

- •
- •
- •
- •
- •
- •

PORT OF DEPARTURE

LOCATION

DATE

TIME

DISTANCE	DURATION

WEATHER CONDITIONS

SEA STRENGTH

CALM 1 2 3 4 5 ROUG

PORT OF DESTINATION

LOCATION

DATE

TIME

PORT INDEX

DOCKMASTER

PHONE

MAIL

DOCKING FEES

SLIP #

SPECIAL FEATURES

ADDITIONAL NOTES

LOGGED BY

BOAT

CAPTAIN

ENGINE HOURS

FUEL

CREW	
•	•
•	•
•	•

PORT OF DEPARTURE

LOCATION

DATE

TIME

DISTANCE	DURATION

WEATHER CONDITIONS

DISTANCE	DURATION

SEA STRENGTH

CALM 1 2 3 4 5 ROUGH

PORT OF DESTINATION

LOCATION

DATE

TIME

PORT INDEX

DOCKMASTER

PHONE

MAIL

DOCKING FEES

SLIP #

SPECIAL FEATURES

ADDITIONAL NOTES

LOGGED BY

BOAT

CAPTAIN

ENGINE HOURS

FUEL

CREW

- •
- •
- •
- •
- •
- •

PORT OF DEPARTURE

LOCATION

DATE

TIME

DISTANCE	DURATION

WEATHER CONDITIONS

SEA STRENGTH

CALM 1 2 3 4 5 ROUGH

PORT OF DESTINATION

LOCATION

DATE

TIME

PORT INDEX

DOCKMASTER

PHONE

MAIL

DOCKING FEES

SLIP #

SPECIAL FEATURES

ADDITIONAL NOTES

LOGGED BY

BOAT

CAPTAIN

ENGINE HOURS

FUEL

CREW

•	•
•	•
•	•

PORT OF DEPARTURE

LOCATION

DATE

TIME

DISTANCE	DURATION

WEATHER CONDITIONS

SEA STRENGTH

CALM 1   2   3   4   5 ROUGH

PORT OF DESTINATION

LOCATION

DATE

TIME

PORT INDEX

DOCKMASTER

PHONE

MAIL

DOCKING FEES

SLIP #

SPECIAL FEATURES

ADDITIONAL NOTES

LOGGED BY

BOAT

CAPTAIN

ENGINE HOURS

FUEL

CREW

•	•
•	•
•	•

PORT OF DEPARTURE

LOCATION

DATE

TIME

DISTANCE	DURATION

PORT OF DESTINATION

LOCATION

DATE

TIME

PORT INDEX

DOCKMASTER

PHONE

MAIL

DOCKING FEES

SLIP #

SPECIAL FEATURES

WEATHER CONDITIONS

SEA STRENGTH

CALM 1 2 3 4 5 ROUGH

ADDITIONAL NOTES

LOGGED BY

BOAT

CAPTAIN

ENGINE HOURS

FUEL

CREW

·	·
·	·
·	·

PORT OF DEPARTURE

LOCATION

DATE

TIME

DISTANCE	DURATION

WEATHER CONDITIONS

SEA STRENGTH

CALM 1 2 3 4 5 ROUGH

PORT OF DESTINATION

LOCATION

DATE

TIME

PORT INDEX

DOCKMASTER

PHONE

MAIL

DOCKING FEES

SLIP #

SPECIAL FEATURES

ADDITIONAL NOTES

LOGGED BY

BOAT

CAPTAIN

ENGINE HOURS

FUEL

CREW

·	·
·	·
·	·

PORT OF DEPARTURE

LOCATION

DATE

TIME

DISTANCE	DURATION

WEATHER CONDITIONS

SEA STRENGTH

CALM ① 1 ② 2 ③ 3 ④ 4 ⑤ 5 ROUGH

PORT OF DESTINATION

LOCATION

DATE

TIME

PORT INDEX

DOCKMASTER

PHONE

MAIL

DOCKING FEES

SLIP #

SPECIAL FEATURES

ADDITIONAL NOTES

LOGGED BY

BOAT

CAPTAIN

ENGINE HOURS

FUEL

CREW

•	•
•	•
•	•

PORT OF DEPARTURE

LOCATION

DATE

TIME

DISTANCE	DURATION

WEATHER CONDITIONS

SEA STRENGTH

CALM 1 2 3 4 5 ROUGH

PORT OF DESTINATION

LOCATION

DATE

TIME

PORT INDEX

DOCKMASTER

PHONE

MAIL

DOCKING FEES

SLIP #

SPECIAL FEATURES

ADDITIONAL NOTES

LOGGED BY

BOAT

CAPTAIN

ENGINE HOURS

FUEL

CREW

-
-
-
-
-
-

PORT OF DEPARTURE

LOCATION

DATE

TIME

DISTANCE	DURATION

WEATHER CONDITIONS

☐	☐	☐	☐	☐

SEA STRENGTH

CALM 1 2 3 4 5 ROUGH

PORT OF DESTINATION

LOCATION

DATE

TIME

PORT INDEX

DOCKMASTER

PHONE

MAIL

DOCKING FEES

SLIP #

SPECIAL FEATURES

ADDITIONAL NOTES

LOGGED BY

BOAT

CAPTAIN

ENGINE HOURS

FUEL

CREW

·	·
·	·
·	·

PORT OF DEPARTURE

LOCATION

DATE

TIME

DISTANCE	DURATION

WEATHER CONDITIONS

SEA STRENGTH

CALM	1	2	3	4	5	ROUGH

PORT OF DESTINATION

LOCATION

DATE

TIME

PORT INDEX

DOCKMASTER

PHONE

MAIL

DOCKING FEES

SLIP #

SPECIAL FEATURES

ADDITIONAL NOTES

LOGGED BY

BOAT

CAPTAIN

ENGINE HOURS

FUEL

CREW

•	•
•	•
•	•

PORT OF DEPARTURE

LOCATION

DATE

TIME

DISTANCE	DURATION

PORT OF DESTINATION

LOCATION

DATE

TIME

PORT INDEX

DOCKMASTER

PHONE

MAIL

DOCKING FEES

SLIP #

SPECIAL FEATURES

WEATHER CONDITIONS

SEA STRENGTH

	1	2	3	4	5	
CALM	○	○	○	○	○	ROUG

ADDITIONAL NOTES

LOGGED BY

BOAT

CAPTAIN

ENGINE HOURS

FUEL

CREW

•	•
•	•
•	•

PORT OF DEPARTURE

LOCATION

DATE

TIME

DISTANCE	DURATION

PORT OF DESTINATION

LOCATION

DATE

TIME

PORT INDEX

DOCKMASTER

PHONE

MAIL

DOCKING FEES

SLIP #

SPECIAL FEATURES

WEATHER CONDITIONS

SEA STRENGTH

CALM   1   2   3   4   5   ROUGH

ADDITIONAL NOTES

LOGGED BY

⛵ BOAT		CREW	
⚙️ CAPTAIN		•	•
🕐 ENGINE HOURS		•	•
🛢️ FUEL		•	•

PORT OF DEPARTURE

📍 LOCATION
📅 DATE
🕐 TIME

DISTANCE	DURATION

WEATHER CONDITIONS

🌡️ —— ☀️ ⛅ 🌧️ ⛈️ ❄️

🚩 —— ☐ ☐ ☐ ☐ ☐

SEA STRENGTH

〜	1	2	3	4	5	〜
CALM	○	○	○	○	○	ROUG

PORT OF DESTINATION

📍 LOCATION
📅 DATE
🕐 TIME

PORT INDEX

🏃 DOCKMASTER
📞 PHONE
✉️ MAIL
💰 DOCKING FEES
⚓ SLIP #
🎖️ SPECIAL FEATURES

ADDITIONAL NOTES

LOGGED BY

BOAT

CAPTAIN

ENGINE HOURS

FUEL

CREW

•	•
•	•
•	•

PORT OF DEPARTURE

LOCATION

DATE

TIME

DISTANCE	DURATION

WEATHER CONDITIONS

SEA STRENGTH

CALM 1 2 3 4 5 ROUGH

PORT OF DESTINATION

LOCATION

DATE

TIME

PORT INDEX

DOCKMASTER

PHONE

MAIL

DOCKING FEES

SLIP #

SPECIAL FEATURES

ADDITIONAL NOTES

LOGGED BY

BOAT

CAPTAIN

ENGINE HOURS

FUEL

CREW

-
-
-
-
-
-

PORT OF DEPARTURE

LOCATION

DATE

TIME

DISTANCE	DURATION

WEATHER CONDITIONS

SEA STRENGTH

CALM 1 2 3 4 5 ROUG

PORT OF DESTINATION

LOCATION

DATE

TIME

PORT INDEX

DOCKMASTER

PHONE

MAIL

DOCKING FEES

SLIP #

SPECIAL FEATURES

ADDITIONAL NOTES

LOGGED BY

BOAT

CAPTAIN

ENGINE HOURS

FUEL

CREW

·	·
·	·
·	·

PORT OF DEPARTURE

LOCATION

DATE

TIME

DISTANCE	DURATION

WEATHER CONDITIONS

SEA STRENGTH

CALM 1 2 3 4 5 ROUGH

PORT OF DESTINATION

LOCATION

DATE

TIME

PORT INDEX

DOCKMASTER

PHONE

MAIL

DOCKING FEES

SLIP #

SPECIAL FEATURES

ADDITIONAL NOTES

LOGGED BY

BOAT

CAPTAIN

ENGINE HOURS

FUEL

CREW

•	•
•	•
•	•

PORT OF DEPARTURE

LOCATION

DATE

TIME

DISTANCE	DURATION

WEATHER CONDITIONS

SEA STRENGTH

CALM   1   2   3   4   5   ROUGH

PORT OF DESTINATION

LOCATION

DATE

TIME

PORT INDEX

DOCKMASTER

PHONE

MAIL

DOCKING FEES

SLIP #

SPECIAL FEATURES

ADDITIONAL NOTES

LOGGED BY

BOAT

CAPTAIN

ENGINE HOURS

FUEL

CREW

•	•
•	•
•	•

PORT OF DEPARTURE

LOCATION

DATE

TIME

DISTANCE	DURATION

WEATHER CONDITIONS

SEA STRENGTH

CALM 1 2 3 4 5 ROUGH

PORT OF DESTINATION

LOCATION

DATE

TIME

PORT INDEX

DOCKMASTER

PHONE

MAIL

DOCKING FEES

SLIP #

SPECIAL FEATURES

ADDITIONAL NOTES

LOGGED BY

BOAT

CAPTAIN

ENGINE HOURS

FUEL

CREW

•	•
•	•
•	•

PORT OF DEPARTURE

LOCATION

DATE

TIME

WEATHER CONDITIONS

DISTANCE	DURATION

SEA STRENGTH

CALM	1	2	3	4	5	ROUG
	○	○	○	○	○	

PORT OF DESTINATION

LOCATION

DATE

TIME

PORT INDEX

DOCKMASTER

PHONE

MAIL

DOCKING FEES

SLIP #

SPECIAL FEATURES

ADDITIONAL NOTES

LOGGED BY

BOAT

⚓ BOAT

⚙ CAPTAIN

🕐 ENGINE HOURS

🛢 FUEL

CREW

•	•
•	•
•	•

PORT OF DEPARTURE

📍 LOCATION

📅 DATE

🕐 TIME

DISTANCE	DURATION

WEATHER CONDITIONS

🌡 ____   ☀ ⛅ 🌧 ⛈ ❄

🏴 ____   ☐ ☐ ☐ ☐ ☐

SEA STRENGTH

CALM 〰 1 ◯ 2 ◯ 3 ◯ 4 ◯ 5 ◯ 🌊 ROUGH

PORT OF DESTINATION

📍 LOCATION

📅 DATE

🕐 TIME

PORT INDEX

🏊 DOCKMASTER

📞 PHONE

✉ MAIL

💲 DOCKING FEES

⚓ SLIP #

🎖 SPECIAL FEATURES

ADDITIONAL NOTES

LOGGED BY

BOAT

CAPTAIN

ENGINE HOURS

FUEL

CREW

•	•
•	•
•	•

PORT OF DEPARTURE

LOCATION

DATE

TIME

DISTANCE	DURATION

WEATHER CONDITIONS

☀ ⛅ 🌧 ⛈ ❄

☐ ☐ ☐ ☐ ☐

SEA STRENGTH

	1	2	3	4	5	
CALM	○	○	○	○	○	ROUGH

PORT OF DESTINATION

LOCATION

DATE

TIME

PORT INDEX

DOCKMASTER

PHONE

MAIL

DOCKING FEES

SLIP #

SPECIAL FEATURES

ADDITIONAL NOTES

LOGGED BY

BOAT

CAPTAIN

ENGINE HOURS

FUEL

CREW

•	•
•	•
•	•

PORT OF DEPARTURE

LOCATION

DATE

TIME

DISTANCE	DURATION

WEATHER CONDITIONS

SEA STRENGTH

CALM 1 2 3 4 5 ROUGH

PORT OF DESTINATION

LOCATION

DATE

TIME

PORT INDEX

DOCKMASTER

PHONE

MAIL

DOCKING FEES

SLIP #

SPECIAL FEATURES

ADDITIONAL NOTES

LOGGED BY

BOAT

CAPTAIN

ENGINE HOURS

FUEL

CREW

-
-
-
-
-
-

PORT OF DEPARTURE

LOCATION

DATE

TIME

DISTANCE	DURATION

WEATHER CONDITIONS

☀ ⛅ 🌧 ⛈ ❄

☐ ☐ ☐ ☐ ☐

SEA STRENGTH

	1	2	3	4	5	
CALM	○	○	○	○	○	ROUGH

PORT OF DESTINATION

LOCATION

DATE

TIME

PORT INDEX

DOCKMASTER

PHONE

MAIL

DOCKING FEES

SLIP #

SPECIAL FEATURES

ADDITIONAL NOTES

LOGGED BY

BOAT

CAPTAIN

ENGINE HOURS

FUEL

CREW

•	•
•	•
•	•

PORT OF DEPARTURE

LOCATION

DATE

TIME

DISTANCE	DURATION

WEATHER CONDITIONS

SEA STRENGTH

CALM 1 2 3 4 5 ROUGH

PORT OF DESTINATION

LOCATION

DATE

TIME

PORT INDEX

DOCKMASTER

PHONE

MAIL

DOCKING FEES

SLIP #

SPECIAL FEATURES

ADDITIONAL NOTES

LOGGED BY

BOAT

CAPTAIN

ENGINE HOURS

FUEL

CREW

•	•
•	•
•	•

PORT OF DEPARTURE

LOCATION

DATE

TIME

DISTANCE	DURATION

WEATHER CONDITIONS

☀ ⛅ ☁ 🌧 ❄

☐ ☐ ☐ ☐ ☐

SEA STRENGTH

	1	2	3	4	5	
CALM	○	○	○	○	○	ROUGH

PORT OF DESTINATION

LOCATION

DATE

TIME

PORT INDEX

DOCKMASTER

PHONE

MAIL

DOCKING FEES

SLIP #

SPECIAL FEATURES

ADDITIONAL NOTES

LOGGED BY

BOAT

CAPTAIN

ENGINE HOURS

FUEL

CREW

•	•
•	•
•	•

PORT OF DEPARTURE

LOCATION

DATE

TIME

DISTANCE	DURATION

WEATHER CONDITIONS

SEA STRENGTH

	1	2	3	4	5	
CALM	◯	◯	◯	◯	◯	ROUGH

PORT OF DESTINATION

LOCATION

DATE

TIME

PORT INDEX

DOCKMASTER

PHONE

MAIL

DOCKING FEES

SLIP #

SPECIAL FEATURES

ADDITIONAL NOTES

LOGGED BY

BOAT

CAPTAIN

ENGINE HOURS

FUEL

CREW

-
-
-
-
-
-

PORT OF DEPARTURE

LOCATION

DATE

TIME

DISTANCE	DURATION

WEATHER CONDITIONS

SEA STRENGTH

	1	2	3	4	5	
CALM	◯	◯	◯	◯	◯	ROU

PORT OF DESTINATION

LOCATION

DATE

TIME

PORT INDEX

DOCKMASTER

PHONE

MAIL

DOCKING FEES

SLIP #

SPECIAL FEATURES

ADDITIONAL NOTES

LOGGED BY

BOAT

CAPTAIN

ENGINE HOURS

FUEL

CREW

•	•
•	•
•	•

PORT OF DEPARTURE

LOCATION

DATE

TIME

DISTANCE	DURATION

PORT OF DESTINATION

LOCATION

DATE

TIME

PORT INDEX

DOCKMASTER

PHONE

MAIL

DOCKING FEES

SLIP #

SPECIAL FEATURES

WEATHER CONDITIONS

SEA STRENGTH

CALM 1 2 3 4 5 ROUGH

ADDITIONAL NOTES

LOGGED BY

BOAT

CAPTAIN

ENGINE HOURS

FUEL

CREW

•	•
•	•
•	•

PORT OF DEPARTURE

LOCATION

DATE

TIME

DISTANCE	DURATION

WEATHER CONDITIONS

SEA STRENGTH

	1	2	3	4	5	
CALM	◯	◯	◯	◯	◯	ROUG

PORT OF DESTINATION

LOCATION

DATE

TIME

PORT INDEX

DOCKMASTER

PHONE

MAIL

DOCKING FEES

SLIP #

SPECIAL FEATURES

ADDITIONAL NOTES

LOGGED BY

BOAT

CAPTAIN

ENGINE HOURS

FUEL

CREW

•	•
•	•
•	•

PORT OF DEPARTURE

LOCATION

DATE

TIME

DISTANCE	DURATION

WEATHER CONDITIONS

SEA STRENGTH

CALM	1	2	3	4	5	ROUGH

PORT OF DESTINATION

LOCATION

DATE

TIME

PORT INDEX

DOCKMASTER

PHONE

MAIL

DOCKING FEES

SLIP #

SPECIAL FEATURES

ADDITIONAL NOTES

LOGGED BY

BOAT

CAPTAIN

ENGINE HOURS

FUEL

CREW

•	•
•	•
•	•

PORT OF DEPARTURE

LOCATION

DATE

TIME

DISTANCE	DURATION

WEATHER CONDITIONS

SEA STRENGTH

CALM 1 2 3 4 5 ROUG

PORT OF DESTINATION

LOCATION

DATE

TIME

PORT INDEX

DOCKMASTER

PHONE

MAIL

DOCKING FEES

SLIP #

SPECIAL FEATURES

ADDITIONAL NOTES

LOGGED BY

BOAT

CAPTAIN

ENGINE HOURS

FUEL

CREW

•	•
•	•
•	•

PORT OF DEPARTURE

LOCATION

DATE

TIME

DISTANCE	DURATION

WEATHER CONDITIONS

☼ ⛅ 🌧 ⛈ ❄

☐ ☐ ☐ ☐ ☐

SEA STRENGTH

CALM 1 2 3 4 5 ROUGH
○ ○ ○ ○ ○

PORT OF DESTINATION

LOCATION

DATE

TIME

PORT INDEX

DOCKMASTER

PHONE

MAIL

DOCKING FEES

SLIP #

SPECIAL FEATURES

ADDITIONAL NOTES

LOGGED BY

BOAT

CAPTAIN

ENGINE HOURS

FUEL

CREW

•	•
•	•
•	•

PORT OF DEPARTURE

LOCATION

DATE

TIME

DISTANCE	DURATION

WEATHER CONDITIONS

SEA STRENGTH

CALM   1   2   3   4   5   ROUG

PORT OF DESTINATION

LOCATION

DATE

TIME

PORT INDEX

DOCKMASTER

PHONE

MAIL

DOCKING FEES

SLIP #

SPECIAL FEATURES

ADDITIONAL NOTES

LOGGED BY

BOAT

CAPTAIN

ENGINE HOURS

FUEL

CREW

•	•
•	•
•	•

PORT OF DEPARTURE

LOCATION

DATE

TIME

DISTANCE	DURATION

WEATHER CONDITIONS

		☀	⛅	🌧	⛈	❄
		☐	☐	☐	☐	☐

SEA STRENGTH

CALM 1 2 3 4 5 ROUGH

PORT OF DESTINATION

LOCATION

DATE

TIME

PORT INDEX

DOCKMASTER

PHONE

MAIL

DOCKING FEES

SLIP #

SPECIAL FEATURES

ADDITIONAL NOTES

LOGGED BY

BOAT

CAPTAIN

ENGINE HOURS

FUEL

CREW

-
-
-
-
-
-

PORT OF DEPARTURE

LOCATION

DATE

TIME

DISTANCE	DURATION

WEATHER CONDITIONS

SEA STRENGTH

CALM 1 2 3 4 5 ROUGH

PORT OF DESTINATION

LOCATION

DATE

TIME

PORT INDEX

DOCKMASTER

PHONE

MAIL

DOCKING FEES

SLIP #

SPECIAL FEATURES

ADDITIONAL NOTES

LOGGED BY

BOAT

CAPTAIN

ENGINE HOURS

FUEL

CREW

•	•
•	•
•	•

PORT OF DEPARTURE

LOCATION

DATE

TIME

DISTANCE	DURATION

WEATHER CONDITIONS

☼ ⛅ 🌧 ⛈ ❄

☐ ☐ ☐ ☐ ☐

SEA STRENGTH

CALM 1 2 3 4 5 ROUGH
○ ○ ○ ○ ○

PORT OF DESTINATION

LOCATION

DATE

TIME

PORT INDEX

DOCKMASTER

PHONE

MAIL

DOCKING FEES

SLIP #

SPECIAL FEATURES

ADDITIONAL NOTES

LOGGED BY

BOAT

CAPTAIN

ENGINE HOURS

FUEL

CREW

•	•
•	•
•	•

PORT OF DEPARTURE

LOCATION

DATE

TIME

DISTANCE	DURATION

WEATHER CONDITIONS

SEA STRENGTH

	1	2	3	4	5	
CALM	○	○	○	○	○	ROUGH

PORT OF DESTINATION

LOCATION

DATE

TIME

PORT INDEX

DOCKMASTER

PHONE

MAIL

DOCKING FEES

SLIP #

SPECIAL FEATURES

ADDITIONAL NOTES

LOGGED BY

BOAT

CAPTAIN

ENGINE HOURS

FUEL

CREW

•	•
•	•
•	•

PORT OF DEPARTURE

LOCATION

DATE

TIME

DISTANCE	DURATION

WEATHER CONDITIONS

SEA STRENGTH

CALM   1   2   3   4   5   ROUGH

PORT OF DESTINATION

LOCATION

DATE

TIME

PORT INDEX

DOCKMASTER

PHONE

MAIL

DOCKING FEES

SLIP #

SPECIAL FEATURES

ADDITIONAL NOTES

LOGGED BY

BOAT

CAPTAIN

ENGINE HOURS

FUEL

CREW

•	•
•	•
•	•

PORT OF DEPARTURE

LOCATION

DATE

TIME

DISTANCE	DURATION

WEATHER CONDITIONS

SEA STRENGTH

	1	2	3	4	5	
CALM	○	○	○	○	○	ROUG

PORT OF DESTINATION

LOCATION

DATE

TIME

PORT INDEX

DOCKMASTER

PHONE

MAIL

DOCKING FEES

SLIP #

SPECIAL FEATURES

ADDITIONAL NOTES

LOGGED BY

BOAT

CAPTAIN

ENGINE HOURS

FUEL

CREW

•	•
•	•
•	•

PORT OF DEPARTURE

LOCATION

DATE

TIME

DISTANCE	DURATION

WEATHER CONDITIONS

SEA STRENGTH

CALM 1 2 3 4 5 ROUGH

PORT OF DESTINATION

LOCATION

DATE

TIME

PORT INDEX

DOCKMASTER

PHONE

MAIL

DOCKING FEES

SLIP #

SPECIAL FEATURES

ADDITIONAL NOTES

LOGGED BY

BOAT

CAPTAIN

ENGINE HOURS

FUEL

CREW

•	•
•	•
•	•

PORT OF DEPARTURE

LOCATION

DATE

TIME

DISTANCE	DURATION

WEATHER CONDITIONS

SEA STRENGTH

CALM 1 2 3 4 5 ROUGH

PORT OF DESTINATION

LOCATION

DATE

TIME

PORT INDEX

DOCKMASTER

PHONE

MAIL

DOCKING FEES

SLIP #

SPECIAL FEATURES

ADDITIONAL NOTES

LOGGED BY

BOAT

CAPTAIN

ENGINE HOURS

FUEL

CREW

•	•
•	•
•	•

PORT OF DEPARTURE

LOCATION

DATE

TIME

DISTANCE	DURATION

WEATHER CONDITIONS

SEA STRENGTH

CALM 1 2 3 4 5 ROUGH

PORT OF DESTINATION

LOCATION

DATE

TIME

PORT INDEX

DOCKMASTER

PHONE

MAIL

DOCKING FEES

SLIP #

SPECIAL FEATURES

ADDITIONAL NOTES

LOGGED BY

⛵ BOAT

⚙️ CAPTAIN

🕐 ENGINE HOURS

FUEL

CREW

- •
- •
- •

- •
- •
- •

PORT OF DEPARTURE

📍 LOCATION

📅 DATE

🕐 TIME

DISTANCE	DURATION

WEATHER CONDITIONS

🌡️ ———

🚩 ———

☀️ ⛅ 🌧️ ⛈️ ❄️

☐ ☐ ☐ ☐ ☐

SEA STRENGTH

CALM	1	2	3	4	5	ROU
	○	○	○	○	○	

PORT OF DESTINATION

📍 LOCATION

📅 DATE

🕐 TIME

PORT INDEX

DOCKMASTER

📞 PHONE

✉️ MAIL

DOCKING FEES

⚓ SLIP #

SPECIAL FEATURES

ADDITIONAL NOTES

LOGGED BY

BOAT

CAPTAIN

ENGINE HOURS

FUEL

CREW

- •
- •
- •
- •
- •
- •

PORT OF DEPARTURE

LOCATION

DATE

TIME

DISTANCE	DURATION

WEATHER CONDITIONS

SEA STRENGTH

CALM 1   2   3   4   5   ROUGH

PORT OF DESTINATION

LOCATION

DATE

TIME

PORT INDEX

DOCKMASTER

PHONE

MAIL

DOCKING FEES

SLIP #

SPECIAL FEATURES

ADDITIONAL NOTES

LOGGED BY

BOAT

CAPTAIN

ENGINE HOURS

FUEL

CREW

•	•
•	•
•	•

PORT OF DEPARTURE

LOCATION

DATE

TIME

DISTANCE	DURATION

WEATHER CONDITIONS

SEA STRENGTH

CALM 1 2 3 4 5 ROUG[H]

PORT OF DESTINATION

LOCATION

DATE

TIME

PORT INDEX

DOCKMASTER

PHONE

MAIL

DOCKING FEES

SLIP #

SPECIAL FEATURES

ADDITIONAL NOTES

LOGGED BY

BOAT

CAPTAIN

ENGINE HOURS

FUEL

CREW

•	•
•	•
•	•

PORT OF DEPARTURE

LOCATION

DATE

TIME

DISTANCE	DURATION

WEATHER CONDITIONS

SEA STRENGTH

CALM 1 2 3 4 5 ROUGH

PORT OF DESTINATION

LOCATION

DATE

TIME

PORT INDEX

DOCKMASTER

PHONE

MAIL

DOCKING FEES

SLIP #

SPECIAL FEATURES

ADDITIONAL NOTES

LOGGED BY

⛵ BOAT

⚙ CAPTAIN

⏱ ENGINE HOURS

🛢 FUEL

CREW

·	·
·	·
·	·

PORT OF DEPARTURE

📍 LOCATION

📅 DATE

🕐 TIME

DISTANCE	DURATION

WEATHER CONDITIONS

🌡 ——   ☀ ⛅ 🌧 ⛈ ❄

🚩 ——   ☐ ☐ ☐ ☐ ☐

SEA STRENGTH

〰 CALM   1 ○   2 ○   3 ○   4 ○   5 ○   ROU

PORT OF DESTINATION

📍 LOCATION

📅 DATE

🕐 TIME

PORT INDEX

🐙 DOCKMASTER

📞 PHONE

✉ MAIL

💲 DOCKING FEES

⚓ SLIP #

🎖 SPECIAL FEATURES

ADDITIONAL NOTES

LOGGED BY

BOAT

CAPTAIN

ENGINE HOURS

FUEL

CREW

•	•
•	•
•	•

PORT OF DEPARTURE

LOCATION

DATE

TIME

DISTANCE	DURATION

WEATHER CONDITIONS

SEA STRENGTH

CALM	1	2	3	4	5	ROUGH

PORT OF DESTINATION

LOCATION

DATE

TIME

PORT INDEX

DOCKMASTER

PHONE

MAIL

DOCKING FEES

SLIP #

SPECIAL FEATURES

ADDITIONAL NOTES

LOGGED BY

⛵ BOAT

⚙ CAPTAIN

🕐 ENGINE HOURS

🛢 FUEL

CREW

•	•
•	•
•	•

PORT OF DEPARTURE

📍 LOCATION

📅 DATE

🕐 TIME

WEATHER CONDITIONS

🌡 ____   ☀ 🌤 🌧 ⛈ ❄

💨 ____   ☐ ☐ ☐ ☐ ☐

DISTANCE	DURATION

SEA STRENGTH

〜 1   2   3   4   5 〜
CALM ◯   ◯   ◯   ◯   ◯ ROUG

PORT OF DESTINATION

📍 LOCATION

📅 DATE

🕐 TIME

PORT INDEX

🏃 DOCKMASTER

📞 PHONE

✉ MAIL

💰 DOCKING FEES

⚓ SLIP #

🎖 SPECIAL FEATURES

ADDITIONAL NOTES

LOGGED BY

BOAT

CAPTAIN

ENGINE HOURS

FUEL

CREW

•	•
•	•
•	•

PORT OF DEPARTURE

LOCATION

DATE

TIME

DISTANCE	DURATION

WEATHER CONDITIONS

SEA STRENGTH

CALM 1 2 3 4 5 ROUGH

PORT OF DESTINATION

LOCATION

DATE

TIME

PORT INDEX

DOCKMASTER

PHONE

MAIL

DOCKING FEES

SLIP #

SPECIAL FEATURES

ADDITIONAL NOTES

LOGGED BY

BOAT

CAPTAIN

ENGINE HOURS

FUEL

CREW

- •
- •
- •
- •
- •
- •

PORT OF DEPARTURE

LOCATION

DATE

TIME

DISTANCE	DURATION

PORT OF DESTINATION

LOCATION

DATE

TIME

PORT INDEX

DOCKMASTER

PHONE

MAIL

DOCKING FEES

SLIP #

SPECIAL FEATURES

WEATHER CONDITIONS

SEA STRENGTH

CALM 1 2 3 4 5 ROUGH

ADDITIONAL NOTES

LOGGED BY

BOAT

CAPTAIN

ENGINE HOURS

FUEL

CREW

·	·
·	·
·	·

PORT OF DEPARTURE

LOCATION

DATE

TIME

DISTANCE	DURATION

WEATHER CONDITIONS

SEA STRENGTH

CALM 1 2 3 4 5 ROUGH

PORT OF DESTINATION

LOCATION

DATE

TIME

PORT INDEX

DOCKMASTER

PHONE

MAIL

DOCKING FEES

SLIP #

SPECIAL FEATURES

ADDITIONAL NOTES

LOGGED BY

BOAT

CAPTAIN

ENGINE HOURS

FUEL

CREW

•	•
•	•
•	•

PORT OF DEPARTURE

LOCATION

DATE

TIME

DISTANCE	DURATION

PORT OF DESTINATION

LOCATION

DATE

TIME

PORT INDEX

DOCKMASTER

PHONE

MAIL

DOCKING FEES

SLIP #

SPECIAL FEATURES

WEATHER CONDITIONS

SEA STRENGTH

CALM 1   2   3   4   5 ROUGH

ADDITIONAL NOTES

LOGGED BY

BOAT

CAPTAIN

ENGINE HOURS

FUEL

CREW

•	•
•	•
•	•

PORT OF DEPARTURE

LOCATION

DATE

TIME

DISTANCE	DURATION

WEATHER CONDITIONS

SEA STRENGTH

CALM 1 2 3 4 5 ROUGH

PORT OF DESTINATION

LOCATION

DATE

TIME

PORT INDEX

DOCKMASTER

PHONE

MAIL

DOCKING FEES

SLIP #

SPECIAL FEATURES

ADDITIONAL NOTES

LOGGED BY

BOAT

CAPTAIN

ENGINE HOURS

FUEL

CREW

-
-
-
-
-
-

PORT OF DEPARTURE

LOCATION

DATE

TIME

DISTANCE	DURATION

WEATHER CONDITIONS

SEA STRENGTH

	1	2	3	4	5	
CALM	○	○	○	○	○	ROUG

PORT OF DESTINATION

LOCATION

DATE

TIME

PORT INDEX

DOCKMASTER

PHONE

MAIL

DOCKING FEES

SLIP #

SPECIAL FEATURES

ADDITIONAL NOTES

LOGGED BY

BOAT

CAPTAIN

ENGINE HOURS

FUEL

CREW

•	•
•	•
•	•

PORT OF DEPARTURE

LOCATION

DATE

TIME

DISTANCE	DURATION

WEATHER CONDITIONS

SEA STRENGTH

CALM 1 2 3 4 5 ROUGH

PORT OF DESTINATION

LOCATION

DATE

TIME

PORT INDEX

DOCKMASTER

PHONE

MAIL

DOCKING FEES

SLIP #

SPECIAL FEATURES

ADDITIONAL NOTES

LOGGED BY

BOAT

CAPTAIN

ENGINE HOURS

FUEL

CREW

•	•
•	•
•	•

PORT OF DEPARTURE

LOCATION

DATE

TIME

DISTANCE	DURATION

WEATHER CONDITIONS

SEA STRENGTH

CALM	1	2	3	4	5	ROUG

PORT OF DESTINATION

LOCATION

DATE

TIME

PORT INDEX

DOCKMASTER

PHONE

MAIL

DOCKING FEES

SLIP #

SPECIAL FEATURES

ADDITIONAL NOTES

LOGGED BY

BOAT

CAPTAIN

ENGINE HOURS

FUEL

CREW

•	•
•	•
•	•

PORT OF DEPARTURE

LOCATION

DATE

TIME

DISTANCE	DURATION

WEATHER CONDITIONS

SEA STRENGTH

CALM 1 2 3 4 5 ROUGH

PORT OF DESTINATION

LOCATION

DATE

TIME

PORT INDEX

DOCKMASTER

PHONE

MAIL

DOCKING FEES

SLIP #

SPECIAL FEATURES

ADDITIONAL NOTES

LOGGED BY

BOAT

CAPTAIN

ENGINE HOURS

FUEL

CREW

-
-
-
-
-
-

PORT OF DEPARTURE

LOCATION

DATE

TIME

DISTANCE	DURATION

WEATHER CONDITIONS

SEA STRENGTH

CALM 1 2 3 4 5 ROUGH

PORT OF DESTINATION

LOCATION

DATE

TIME

PORT INDEX

DOCKMASTER

PHONE

MAIL

DOCKING FEES

SLIP #

SPECIAL FEATURES

ADDITIONAL NOTES

LOGGED BY

BOAT

CAPTAIN

ENGINE HOURS

FUEL

CREW

•	•
•	•
•	•

PORT OF DEPARTURE

LOCATION

DATE

TIME

DISTANCE	DURATION

WEATHER CONDITIONS

SEA STRENGTH

CALM 1 2 3 4 5 ROUGH

PORT OF DESTINATION

LOCATION

DATE

TIME

PORT INDEX

DOCKMASTER

PHONE

MAIL

DOCKING FEES

SLIP #

SPECIAL FEATURES

ADDITIONAL NOTES

LOGGED BY

BOAT

CAPTAIN

ENGINE HOURS

FUEL

CREW

- •
- •
- •
- •
- •
- •

PORT OF DEPARTURE

LOCATION

DATE

TIME

DISTANCE	DURATION

WEATHER CONDITIONS

☀ ⛅ 🌧 ⛈ ❄
☐ ☐ ☐ ☐ ☐

SEA STRENGTH

CALM 1 2 3 4 5 ROUGH

PORT OF DESTINATION

LOCATION

DATE

TIME

PORT INDEX

DOCKMASTER

PHONE

MAIL

DOCKING FEES

SLIP #

SPECIAL FEATURES

ADDITIONAL NOTES

LOGGED BY

BOAT

CAPTAIN

ENGINE HOURS

FUEL

CREW

•	•
•	•
•	•

PORT OF DEPARTURE

LOCATION

DATE

TIME

DISTANCE	DURATION

WEATHER CONDITIONS

SEA STRENGTH

CALM 1 2 3 4 5 ROUGH

PORT OF DESTINATION

LOCATION

DATE

TIME

PORT INDEX

DOCKMASTER

PHONE

MAIL

DOCKING FEES

SLIP #

SPECIAL FEATURES

ADDITIONAL NOTES

LOGGED BY

BOAT

CAPTAIN

ENGINE HOURS

FUEL

CREW

-
-
-
-
-
-

PORT OF DEPARTURE

LOCATION

DATE

TIME

DISTANCE	DURATION

WEATHER CONDITIONS

SEA STRENGTH

CALM   1   2   3   4   5   ROUGH

PORT OF DESTINATION

LOCATION

DATE

TIME

PORT INDEX

DOCKMASTER

PHONE

MAIL

DOCKING FEES

SLIP #

SPECIAL FEATURES

ADDITIONAL NOTES

LOGGED BY

BOAT

CAPTAIN

ENGINE HOURS

FUEL

CREW

•	•
•	•
•	•

PORT OF DEPARTURE

LOCATION

DATE

TIME

DISTANCE	DURATION

WEATHER CONDITIONS

SEA STRENGTH

CALM 1 2 3 4 5 ROUGH

PORT OF DESTINATION

LOCATION

DATE

TIME

PORT INDEX

DOCKMASTER

PHONE

MAIL

DOCKING FEES

SLIP #

SPECIAL FEATURES

ADDITIONAL NOTES

LOGGED BY

BOAT

CAPTAIN

ENGINE HOURS

FUEL

CREW

·	·
·	·
·	·

PORT OF DEPARTURE

LOCATION

DATE

TIME

WEATHER CONDITIONS

SEA STRENGTH

	1	2	3	4	5	
CALM	◯	◯	◯	◯	◯	ROUG

DISTANCE	DURATION

PORT OF DESTINATION

LOCATION

DATE

TIME

PORT INDEX

DOCKMASTER

PHONE

MAIL

DOCKING FEES

SLIP #

SPECIAL FEATURES

ADDITIONAL NOTES

LOGGED BY

BOAT

CAPTAIN

ENGINE HOURS

FUEL

CREW

•	•
•	•
•	•

PORT OF DEPARTURE

LOCATION

DATE

TIME

DISTANCE	DURATION

WEATHER CONDITIONS

SEA STRENGTH

CALM   1   2   3   4   5   ROUGH

PORT OF DESTINATION

LOCATION

DATE

TIME

PORT INDEX

DOCKMASTER

PHONE

MAIL

DOCKING FEES

SLIP #

SPECIAL FEATURES

ADDITIONAL NOTES

LOGGED BY

BOAT

CAPTAIN

ENGINE HOURS

FUEL

CREW

•	•
•	•
•	•

PORT OF DEPARTURE

LOCATION

DATE

TIME

DISTANCE	DURATION

WEATHER CONDITIONS

SEA STRENGTH

CALM 1 2 3 4 5 ROUGH

PORT OF DESTINATION

LOCATION

DATE

TIME

PORT INDEX

DOCKMASTER

PHONE

MAIL

DOCKING FEES

SLIP #

SPECIAL FEATURES

ADDITIONAL NOTES

LOGGED BY

BOAT

CAPTAIN

ENGINE HOURS

FUEL

CREW

•	•
•	•
•	•

PORT OF DEPARTURE

LOCATION

DATE

TIME

DISTANCE	DURATION

WEATHER CONDITIONS

SEA STRENGTH

	1	2	3	4	5	
CALM	○	○	○	○	○	ROUGH

PORT OF DESTINATION

LOCATION

DATE

TIME

PORT INDEX

DOCKMASTER

PHONE

MAIL

DOCKING FEES

SLIP #

SPECIAL FEATURES

ADDITIONAL NOTES

LOGGED BY

BOAT

CAPTAIN

ENGINE HOURS

FUEL

CREW

•	•
•	•
•	•

PORT OF DEPARTURE

LOCATION

DATE

TIME

DISTANCE	DURATION

WEATHER CONDITIONS

SEA STRENGTH

CALM 1 2 3 4 5 ROUGH

PORT OF DESTINATION

LOCATION

DATE

TIME

PORT INDEX

DOCKMASTER

PHONE

MAIL

DOCKING FEES

SLIP #

SPECIAL FEATURES

ADDITIONAL NOTES

LOGGED BY

BOAT

CAPTAIN

ENGINE HOURS

FUEL

CREW

•	•
•	•
•	•

PORT OF DEPARTURE

LOCATION

DATE

TIME

DISTANCE	DURATION

WEATHER CONDITIONS

SEA STRENGTH

CALM 1 2 3 4 5 ROUGH

PORT OF DESTINATION

LOCATION

DATE

TIME

PORT INDEX

DOCKMASTER

PHONE

MAIL

DOCKING FEES

SLIP #

SPECIAL FEATURES

ADDITIONAL NOTES

LOGGED BY

BOAT

CAPTAIN

ENGINE HOURS

FUEL

CREW

•	•
•	•
•	•

PORT OF DEPARTURE

LOCATION

DATE

TIME

DISTANCE	DURATION

WEATHER CONDITIONS

SEA STRENGTH

CALM	1	2	3	4	5	ROUG

PORT OF DESTINATION

LOCATION

DATE

TIME

PORT INDEX

DOCKMASTER

PHONE

MAIL

DOCKING FEES

SLIP #

SPECIAL FEATURES

ADDITIONAL NOTES

LOGGED BY

BOAT

CAPTAIN

ENGINE HOURS

FUEL

CREW

•	•
•	•
•	•

PORT OF DEPARTURE

LOCATION

DATE

TIME

DISTANCE	DURATION

PORT OF DESTINATION

LOCATION

DATE

TIME

PORT INDEX

DOCKMASTER

PHONE

MAIL

DOCKING FEES

SLIP #

SPECIAL FEATURES

WEATHER CONDITIONS

SEA STRENGTH

CALM   1   2   3   4   5   ROUGH

ADDITIONAL NOTES

LOGGED BY

BOAT

CAPTAIN

ENGINE HOURS

FUEL

CREW

•	•
•	•
•	•

PORT OF DEPARTURE

LOCATION

DATE

TIME

DISTANCE	DURATION

WEATHER CONDITIONS

SEA STRENGTH

CALM 1 2 3 4 5 ROUG

PORT OF DESTINATION

LOCATION

DATE

TIME

PORT INDEX

DOCKMASTER

PHONE

MAIL

DOCKING FEES

SLIP #

SPECIAL FEATURES

ADDITIONAL NOTES

LOGGED BY

BOAT

CAPTAIN

ENGINE HOURS

FUEL

CREW

•	•
•	•
•	•

PORT OF DEPARTURE

LOCATION

DATE

TIME

DISTANCE	DURATION

WEATHER CONDITIONS

🌡 ___	☀	⛅	☁	🌧	❄
🚩 ___	☐	☐	☐	☐	☐

SEA STRENGTH

CALM 1 2 3 4 5 ROUGH

PORT OF DESTINATION

LOCATION

DATE

TIME

PORT INDEX

DOCKMASTER

PHONE

MAIL

DOCKING FEES

SLIP #

SPECIAL FEATURES

ADDITIONAL NOTES

LOGGED BY